Blastoff! Readers are carefully developed by literacy experts to build reading stamina and move students toward fluency by combining standards-based content with developmentally appropriate text.

 Level 1 provides the most support through repetition of high-frequency words, light text, predictable sentence patterns, and strong visual support.

 Level 2 offers early readers a bit more challenge through varied sentences, increased text load, and text-supportive special features.

 Level 3 advances early-fluent readers toward fluency through increased text load, less reliance on photos, advancing concepts, longer sentences, and more complex special features.

★ **Blastoff! Universe**

Reading Level

This edition first published in 2026 by Bellwether Media, Inc.

No part of this publication may be reproduced in whole or in part without written permission of the publisher. For information regarding permission, write to Bellwether Media, Inc., Attention: Permissions Department, 3500 American Blvd W, Suite 150, Bloomington, MN 55431.

Library of Congress Cataloging-in-Publication Data

Names: Langdo, Bryan author
Title: Iceland / by Bryan Langdo.
Description: Minneapolis : Bellwether Media, Inc, 2026. | Series: Countries of the world | "Blastoff Readers 2"–Cover. | Includes bibliographical references and index. | Audience: Ages 5-8 | Audience: Grades 2-3 | Summary: "Relevant images match informative text in this introduction to Iceland. Intended for students in kindergarten through third grade" – Provided by publisher.
Identifiers: LCCN 2025015009 (print) | LCCN 2025015010 (ebook) | ISBN 9798893044591 library binding | ISBN 9798893045970 ebook
Subjects: LCSH: Iceland-Juvenile literature
Classification: LCC DL305 .L36 2026 (print) | LCC DL305 (ebook) | DDC 949.12–dc23/eng/20250403
LC record available at https://lccn.loc.gov/2025015009
LC ebook record available at https://lccn.loc.gov/2025015010

Text copyright © 2026 by Bellwether Media, Inc. BLASTOFF! READERS and associated logos are trademarks and/or registered trademarks of Bellwether Media, Inc. Bellwether Media is a division of FlutterBee Education Group.

Editor: Betsy Rathburn   Designer: Laura Sowers

Printed in the United States of America, North Mankato, MN.

Table of Contents

All About Iceland	4
Land and Animals	6
Life in Iceland	12
Iceland Facts	20
Glossary	22
To Learn More	23
Index	24

All About Iceland

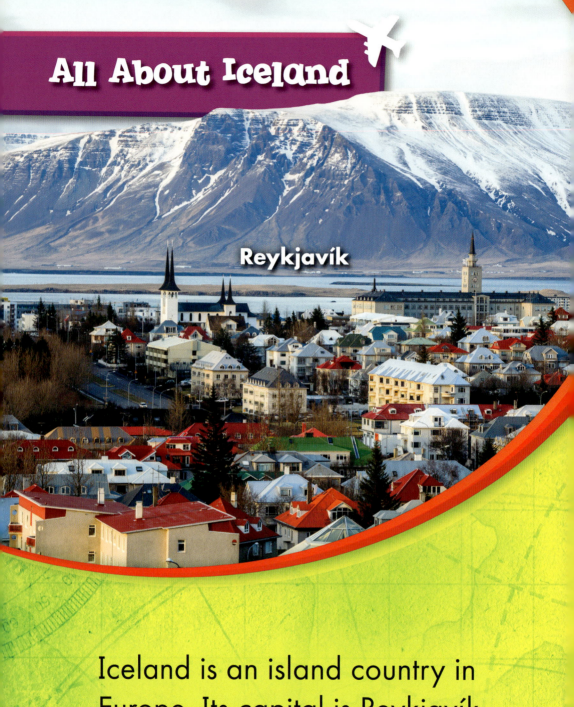

Reykjavík

Iceland is an island country in Europe. Its capital is Reykjavík.

Iceland has many **volcanoes** and **glaciers**. It is called the Land of Fire and Ice!

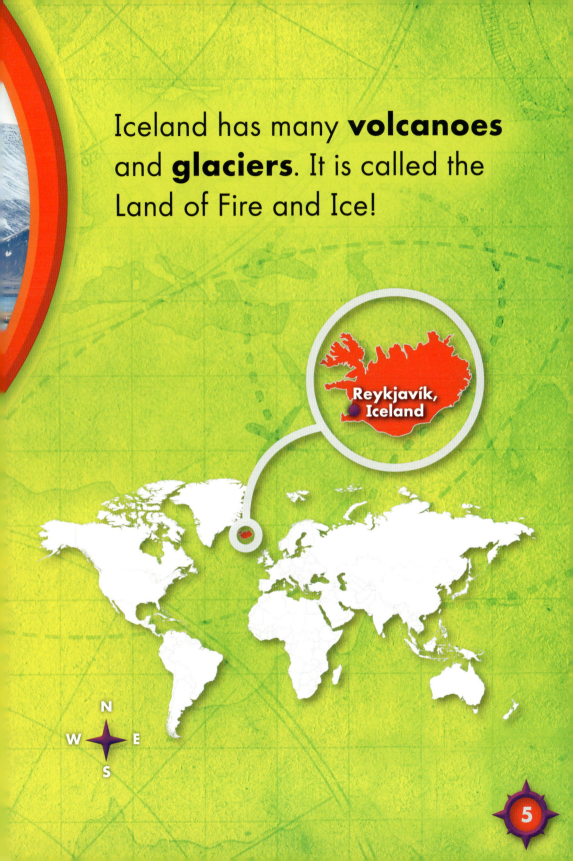

Land and Animals

The Atlantic Ocean surrounds Iceland. **Fjords** line much of the coast.

Mountains rise in the middle. The southwest is dotted with **geysers**. Waterfalls spill over cliffs.

fjord

Skógafoss

Size: 197 feet (60 meters) tall

Famous For: one of Iceland's most famous waterfalls

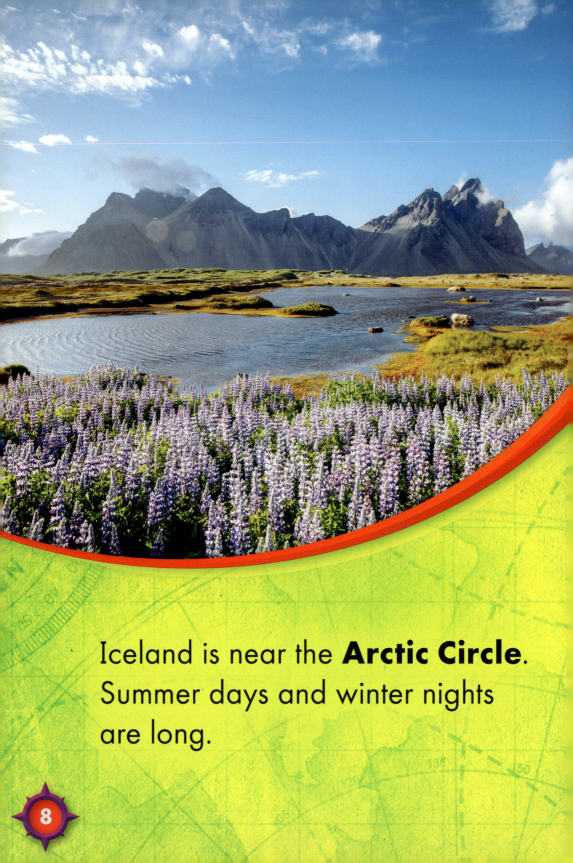

Iceland is near the **Arctic Circle**. Summer days and winter nights are long.

The north has colder winters than the south. The Northern Lights often light the sky!

Northern Lights

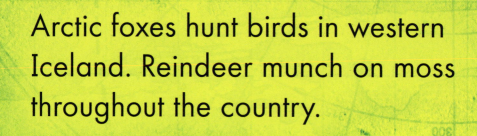

Arctic foxes hunt birds in western Iceland. Reindeer munch on moss throughout the country.

reindeer

Animals of Iceland

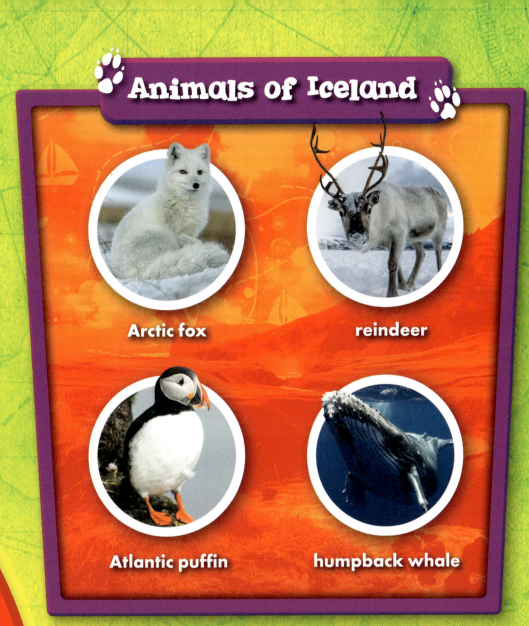

Arctic fox

reindeer

Atlantic puffin

humpback whale

Puffins make nests on **coastal** cliffs. Whales swim in the ocean.

Life in Iceland

Most people in Iceland have an Icelandic **background**. Icelandic is the main language.

Most people live along the coast. About half live in Reykjavík.

Icelandic horses

reading

Reading is popular in Iceland. Concerts are popular, too.

Many people play soccer. Some like to ride Icelandic horses. To relax, people swim in **hot springs**.

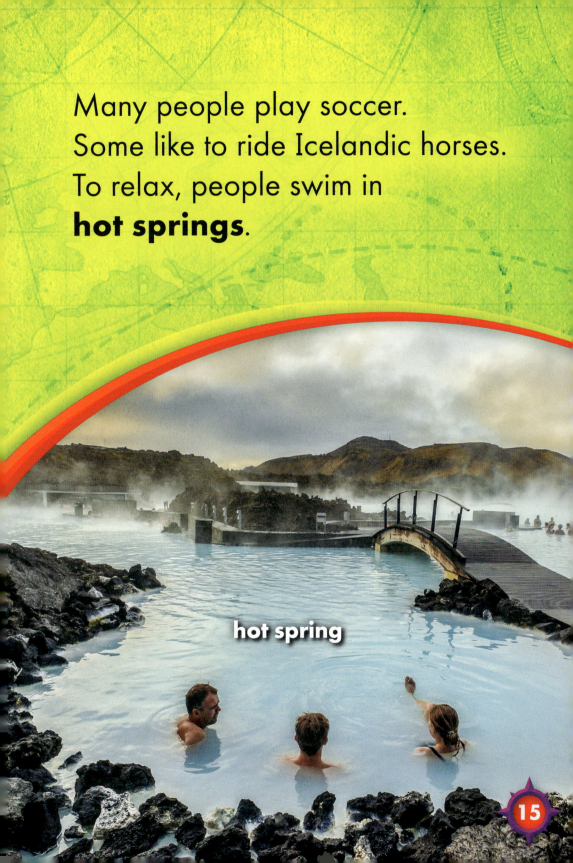

hot spring

Icelanders eat a lot of lamb and fish. Skyr is yogurt that many people eat for breakfast.

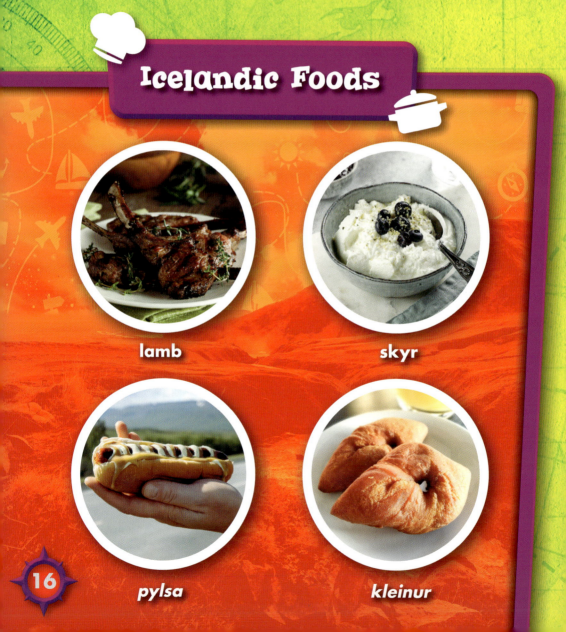

Icelandic Foods

lamb

skyr

pylsa

kleinur

Pylsa are Icelandic hot dogs.
Kleinur are fried donuts.

June 17 is National Day. People **celebrate** with parades and concerts.

The Viking **Festival** also happens in June. People act out battles. Icelanders love their **heritage**!

National Day

Viking Festival

Iceland Facts

Size:
39,769 square miles
(103,000 square kilometers)

Population:
364,036 (2024)

National Holiday:
National Day (June 17)

Main Language:
Icelandic

Capital City:
Reykjavík

Famous Face

Name: Björk

Famous For: award-winning singer, songwriter, and actress

Religions

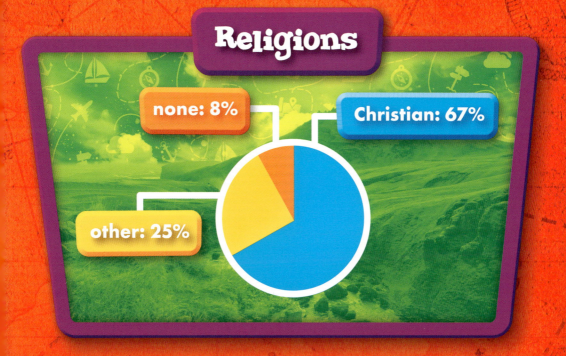

none: 8%
Christian: 67%
other: 25%

Top Landmarks

Blue Lagoon

Hallgrímskirkja

Thingvellir National Park

Glossary

Arctic Circle—an imaginary line that circles the top of the globe, parallel to the equator

background—people's experiences, knowledge, and family history

celebrate—to do something special or fun for an event, occasion, or holiday

coastal—near the shore

festival—a time or event of celebration

fjords—narrow inlets from the sea between cliffs or steep slopes

geysers—springs that sometimes spray hot water and steam

glaciers—massive sheets of ice that cover large areas of land

heritage—the backgrounds and beliefs that are part of the history of a group of people

hot springs—places where warm water flows out of the ground

volcanoes—holes in the earth; when a volcano erupts, hot ash, gas, or melted rock called lava shoots out.

To Learn More

AT THE LIBRARY

Hubbard, Ben. *Welcome to Iceland.* New York, N.Y.: DK Publishing, 2021.

Laboucarie, Sandra. *Volcanoes.* San Francisco, Calif.: Chronicle Books, 2022.

McKay, C.R. *Iceland.* New York, N.Y.: Cavendish Square Publishing, 2022.

ON THE WEB

FACTSURFER

Factsurfer.com gives you a safe, fun way to find more information.

1. Go to www.factsurfer.com.
2. Enter "Iceland" into the search box and click 🔍.
3. Select your book cover to see a list of related content.

Index

animals, 10, 11, 15
Arctic Circle, 8
Atlantic Ocean, 6, 11
capital (see Reykjavík)
cliffs, 6, 11
coast, 6, 11, 12
concerts, 14, 18
Europe, 4
fjords, 6
food, 16, 17
geysers, 6
glaciers, 5
hot springs, 15
Iceland facts, 20–21
Icelandic, 12, 13
island, 4
map, 5
mountains, 6

National Day, 18
Northern Lights, 9
people, 12, 15, 16, 18
reading, 14
Reykjavík, 4, 5, 12
say hello, 13
Skógafoss, 7
soccer, 15
summer, 8
Viking Festival, 18, 19
volcanoes, 5
waterfalls, 6, 7
winter, 8, 9

The images in this book are reproduced through the courtesy of: clkraus, front cover; em_concepts, p. 3; Boyloso, pp. 4-5; Mumemories, p. 6; Lowpower, pp. 6-7; Creative Travel Projects, pp. 8-9; Piotr Krzeslak, p. 9; Masasemi Photography, pp. 10-11; Alexey Seafarer, p. 11 (Arctic fox); Pav-Pro Photography Ltd, p. 11 (reindeer); Kamil Kubalik, p. 11 (Atlantic puffin); Kertu, p. 11 (humpback whale); canadastock, p. 12; wilpunt, pp. 12-13; Abinieks, p. 14 (Icelandic horses); LukaTDB, p. 14 (reading); weniliou, pp. 14-15; Brent Hofacker, p. 16 (lamb); RomanaMart, p. 16 (*skyr*); FotoHelin, p. 16 (*pylsa*); Pom Bakery, p. 16 (*kleinur*); Icelandic photo agency/ Alamy Stock Photo, p. 17; RnDmS, p. 18; Atis Eversss, pp. 18-19; Hybrid Gfx, p. 20 (flag); Records/ Alamy Stock Photo, p. 20 (Björk); Puripat Lertpunyaroj, p. 21 (Blue Lagoon); MisterStock, p. 21 (Hallgrímskirkja); Alexey Stiop, p. 21 (Thingvellir National Park); FotoRequest, p. 22.

24